The Colour of My Dreams

Peter Dixon is a full-time writer and performer visiting schools, festivals and more or less anywhere between Munchen Gladbach and glorious St Ives. Peter hasn't got a Labrador, or a computer, but he does have a pond, a wife, three grandchildren, a Southampton season ticket and a tortoise called Flash.

David Thomas teaches art at a sixth-form college in Winchester. His outlook on life has been shaped by four years living in Japan, twenty-eight years mowing his lawn and fifty-eight years avoiding sunstroke. The *Colour of My Dreams* is the seventh Peter Dixon book he has illustrated.

The Colour of My Dreams

Illustrated by David Thomas

MACMILLAN CHILDREN'S BOOKS

To Marion,
who made it happen

First published 2002 by Macmillan Children's Books

This edition published 2008 by Macmillan Children's Books
a division of Macmillan Publishers Limited
20 New Wharf Road, London N1 9RR
Basingstoke and Oxford
Associated companies throughout the world
www.panmacmillan.com

ISBN 978-0-330-46964-7

Text copyright © Peter Dixon 2002
Illustrations copyright © David Thompson 2002

The right of Peter Dixon and David Thompson to be identified
as the author and illustrator of this work has been asserted by them
in accordance with the Copyright, Designs and Patents Act 1988.

1 3 5 7 9 8 6 4 2

A CIP catalogue record for this book is available from
the British Library.

Printed and bound in the UK by CPI Mackays, Chatham ME5 8TD

A recent visit to Naomi House Children's Hospice inspired Razorlight drummer Andy Burrows to release an album in aid of the charity. He approached Peter, whom he has known since childhood, and asked to use some of the poems in this book as lyrics. Proceeds from the sale of this book and the album of the same name are going to help build Jack's Place – a new wing of the hospice providing care for older children.

Here's what Peter says:

I like dreaming and playing with words – those that rhyme and those that don't. I like playing with friends who helped me make this book, and with people who made the CD happen.

Pals like David Thomas, Gaby Morgan, Andy Burrows and Reg the dog. Except for Gaby, who plays with cats and dwelt somewhere else, we all lived in the same road. Dave lives at number 41 with his scratchy pen and blobby ink, I live at number 30 without a computer, and Andy used to live at number 49. When I pass Andy's old house on my way to post a letter, I can (almost) hear him practising and practising and practising his bedroom drumming. Andy used to play with my dog, Reg, but now he plays with Razorlight instead.

Peter Dixon

To Marion
Who made it happen

Contents

Pockets

Poet's pocket ——— paper pen,
Farmer's pocket —— speckled hen,
Pirate's pocket —— gold doubloon,
Lover's pocket —— lover's moon,
Robber's pocket —— ten long years,
Hunter's pocket —— blood and tears,
Sailor's pocket —— salty tales,
Winter's pocket —— wind and gales,
Poacher's pocket —— rabbit snare,
Mother's pocket —— love and care,
Rich man's pocket — bacon rolls,
Poor man's pocket — husks and holes

Angels

I have not seen many angels
this year
     . . . not proper ones
    not the kind that are born
    every time a bell rings
    or a baby dies.
I have seen plenty in paintings
    plastic and stone
    ones made of silver
    in crystal or gold.
I've seen steel on a hillside
    marble in church
    wood in the chancel
    iron on a grave.
But not a proper one,
not the real ones sent to guard us
as we sleep.
I've not seen an angel's feather
by my bedside for a long time.
Not since we threw away
the eiderdown.

Isobel

A poem for a small girl,
whose daddy did not fix
the cage door properly.

On my evening stroll
through the land of small furry creatures
I am pleased to report
upon
having
met Stan.
      You will
      doubtless
      be pleased to hear
           that he has been made king
           of lost hamsters . . .
wears a crown
and enjoys a
new
spacious cage
complete with
correctly maintained
door.
And as a welcoming gift from his new furry friends
a splendid
      Ferret Wheel.

Whiskers in the Clouds

Do not weep for Whiskers
he has his new warm home
eiderdowns of softness
pillows linen white.
He purrrrrrrs in evening suntime
    – sleeps by day
      and night –
          Whisker's dreams are happy
          and
          Whisker's quite
          all right.

Drummer Boy

*In olden days it was thought lucky to spit
on the drummer's hand before battle.*

Hear the drum boy tapping
beside the corporal's fire.
Hear the ensign whistle,
Hear the sergeant sing.
Watch the shadows dancing,
see the steel of dawn.
Hear the major's orders,
hear the soldiers swear.
> Hear the clip of bayonet,
> see them standing calm,
> watch them prime their muskets
> and spit the drummer's palm.
Hear them curse the ballshot,
see them hold their line,
safe behind sweet Jesus
and the drummer's palm.
> Hear their final volley
> pipeclayed soldiers
> stand . . .
a drum
a boy, so silent,
spittle on his hand.

Beware

Do not go to the bottom of the garden,
my lovelies,
always take a care.
Do not go to the bottom of the garden,
children,
there is nothing for you there.
Stay close beside the rosebed
Stay close beside the wall,
the garden way is watching
so do not laugh or call.
Stay close together,
darlings,
             oh please,
        oh please, beware
        . . . hold your shadows tightly
        look –
             but never stare.

Heroes

Rupert
Keats
and Nelson
. . . heroes old and new
I could list them in all colours
I could list them all
for you.
There are tons and tons of heroes
but mine's a SUPER one.
She isn't very famous,
and she is called
My mum!

Moon

Last night
I noticed
a small piece
missing
from the moon . . .
Not a big piece
just a small piece
  and perhaps we need not care –
  But a small piece isn't shining
  and a small piece
  isn't there.

Last Summer Leaf

Summer leaf
summer leaf
reach for the sky.
Your summer has ended
so why don't you fly?
Put on your jacket
of scarlet and rust
buttons of ochre
ruffles of crust.
Fly from your tree top,
flee summer's hand:
it's time to weave carpets
and paint your new land.

Missionary Sales

*This poem is about my grandma who lived
in Liverton Mines*

By Yorkshire coals
and mantled light
she wove her carpets
night by night . . .
glint of scissors
hook and peg
twist of finger
nod of head.
I see her shadow
days gone by
sigh of body
squint of eye
     . . . thrums of scarlet
     gold and blue
     mats for God
     in Timbuktoo.

I'm Not Scared of Anything

I'm not scared of ANYTHING
well – only dogs and cats
bats and rats
and things that scratch
and things that hop or crawl.
No, I'm not scared of ANYTHING
well – only birds a bit
worms that squirm
fires that burn
and big boys in the park.

I'm not even scared of darkness
I sleep alone, each night
my teddy gives me cuddles
if I switch off the light.

I'm really very brave, you see
I'm big and brave and strong,
–
   the only thing that frightens me
   is getting spellings
   rong.

First Assembly

Teacher says that this morning
we are going to our first
Assembly.
I don't want to go to Assembly.
I didn't like the Tower of London much.
I won't like Assembly.
I have not got my money.
I have not got my packed lunch
or my swimming things . . .
And I don't want to go to Assembly.
I want to stay here in my new school.
I like my new school
I like my new teacher
I like my new friends
and the gerbil.
     I want to stay here.
     Anyway –
          I can't go to Assembly
          because
          mum's collecting me after school
          and we are going straight to
          Tescos.

R.I.P.

Flies that die on window panes
have no crosses
have no graves.
No epitaph to state their name
as aces of the flying game.
No name neat etched in stone or brass
to tell a death on walls of glass.
Just crispen pyres,
piled
currant black.
Here lies a fallen acrobat.

Stamp Licker

Peter licked a postage stamp
and thought
this tastes quite nice
so he sprinkled it with pepper
and a little bit of rice.

He garnished it with garlic
some peanuts and some ham
a little bit of liver
and a little blob of jam.
He stirred it up with custard
some tea and Perrin's sauce
and served it up at dinner
for father's second course!

'Yum yum!'
said Peter's daddy
'This tastes like something new.'
'It is,' smiled clever Peter
'and I made it just for you!'

Lost Voice

Our teacher lost her voice
today . . .
    We don't know where it's gone,
we've searched all round the classroom
and all round the hall.

We've searched inside the cupboard,
we've looked behind the wall
and even in the toilets . . .
    It can't be found at all!

My mother says it's dreadful
my mother says it's sad . . .
    Miss Johnson only
    whispers
But we are rather glad.

The World's First Goal

In the days of Stone Age people
a long, long time ago
a man invented football
and his name was –
           Stone Age Joe.

Joe made the world's first football
he carved it out of stone
his boots were made of granite
and the goalposts built of bone.

He called his team The Stoners
Joe was their number nine
antlers for the corners
pebbles for the lines.

Joe's name is everlasting
for he scored the world's first goal
in a match against United
– but it took a dreadful toll.
A cross came from the Winger
a chap called Stone Age Ted
brave Joe he rose to meet it
and hit it with his head!
'Goooooooaaaaaaaaaaaaaalllll . . .'
yelled all the cave folk
'Well done!' cried speedy Ted
But Joe's career was over
for Joe was stone-cold
           dead.

They built a grand memorial
to Joe who headed rocks
a football carved of
flint stone
 and a pair of
Stone Age socks.

His name will live for ever
upon the players' role
the man who started football
and scored
the greatest goal.

Poetry Cook

A pinch of time
    or rhythm
a dash of haiku too
half a cup of kenning
and just a splosh of rhyme,
sonnet it quite slowly
serve with cinquained dove
and always
    always
    always
    clerihew
    with love.

Problem Solving

Our teacher likes to
solve problems.
But I don't like
solving problems.
That's my problem.
I would like to invent
a way to make my teacher
disappear.
I try hard
but cannot find the right solution.

Winter

Winter, winter
hear the roar
bangs our window
bangs our door.
Bites our fingers
bites our toes
nips our ears
nips our nose.
Horrid winter
dreadful jaws
coughs and sniffles
spits and roars.
We hate winter
'Go away'
except (perhaps)
on Christmas Day.

Christmas
Christmas, fires and firs
listen
listen
winter purrrrrs.

Peace

*A poem written after watching Oliver
examining a dead fly*

Hands together
    nice and neat
showman's jacket
    folded feet . . .
Little fly
    now you're dead,
    can I stroke your tiny head?
    Let me touch your fairy wings,
    nose and feet
    and other things.
Autumn fly
    I watched you dance,
    wall and window
    flower and branch.
Your summer's gone,
your hours have flown.
Let me gently take you home.

Little Pools

Just behind the sofa
and pictures on the wall
live little pools of darkness
– mostly very small . . .
They hide there in the daytime
they follow me to bed
and fill my room with darkness
when I lay down
my head.

Tom Thumb

Tom Thumb's my super-hero
so stand him in the town.
His head –
    a wreath of laurel
    his head a golden crown.
I'd really like to see him,
a reminder to us all
that children can be
heroes . . .
    the poor
    the weak
    and small.

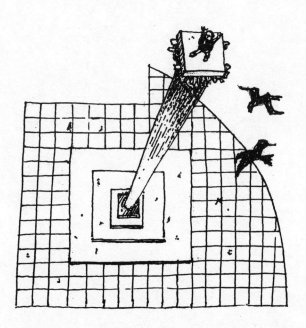

Last Patrol

September wasps remind me of fighter pilots.

Last patrol
Goggle-eyed
and tiger garbed
heroes of a hundred days . . .
    they mass
More of instinct than intent.
More in duty than of war.
Guardians of a rusting crop.

In orchard skies
and frost-fringed days
they fly.

The last of the many.

Lighthouse Men 1

Big and tall
don't have to
climb
up
steps
at
all.

But stand
with
candles
on
their
head.

Sometimes
green
and
sometimes
RED.

Lighthouse Men II

Lighthouse keepers
who are small
Can't be seen by
boats at all

But:
when they
stand
on piles of
boxes
boats sail
safely

     past the
     rocksies.

Parents' Evening

I always hated parents' evenings. Parents can be so embarrassing.

Mrs Flurry	comes in late,
	dressed up like a garden fête
Mr Stalky	tall and thin
	funny nose, great big chin
Dipti's mother	likes to laugh
Robert's father	simply daft
Mr Dobson	big tattoos
Mrs Dobson	really cool
Darren's family	football crazy
Freddie's family	looking lazy
Lorna's father	moans and moans
Lorna's mother	phones and phones
Mr Smedley	horrid shirt
Mrs Smedley	dreadful skirt
Wesley's mother	waves and calls
Mr Hobson	trips and falls
See my mother?	
See my dad?	
	They've stayed at home –
I'm really glad.	

Seagulls

Some grown-ups moan about everything being
dangerous — even conker trees and birds.

Let's rid the world of seagulls
let's rid the sea of gulls
messy, squawky creatures
with nests
and baby gulls.

Let's rid the land of insects
wasp nests, smelly ponds
things that sting or itch us
things that don't look nice.

Let's chop down trees that darken
block our view or sway
drop sticky stuff on motors
– or just get in the way.

Let's make our world a safe one
keep nature locked in jars
    – our world could be so lovely
    if it was just
            bricks
            and
            cars.

Cuddle

I'd rather have a cuddle
than a video,
I'd rather have a cuddle
than anything I know,
I'd rather have a cuddle
than ketchup, chips or peas,
a computer can be lovely
but –
a cuddle's what I need.

Shadow Collector

On summer afternoons
    sometimes evenings
I collect shadows . . .
    mainly people
    but sometimes cats and dogs.
I store them away
nice and flat
carefully ironed
between sheets of softest paper,
    free from light
    and prowling shadow thieves.
I collect my shadows from walls and
pavements
    playground spaces
    beaches
    streets
    and gloomy places . . .
Old-folk shadows
young and poor
teachers' shadows
(classroom floors).
But one is special
It's big.
It's tall

And I found it on a palace wall.

Bathtime

Bathtime
       lark time
       plastic shark time
       fish and mermaids
       purple ducks.
Bathtime
       laugh time
       really daft time
       screams and wiggles
       coughs and spits.
Bathtime
       bed time
       soon be mine time
       when Dad's finished
       I'll get in.

Memories

On the pier
   old pirates
      laugh and spit
         swig rum
            shout 'yo-ho-ho'
and re-fight yesterday's battles.

In the park
   yesterday's teachers
      moan and groan
         sip tea
            read work sheets
and catch up on last year's marking.

Dad's Tale

Before the days of pet food
when dogs were thin and wild,
my grandma lost a baby
my grandma lost a child.
Stray dogs snatched her baby
They stole him from her bed . . .
and took him to a forest
where woodmen feared to tread.
They built a nest of elderwood,
they fed him squirrel tails,
showed him where the chickens hid
and taught him poachers' trails.
They taught him all their moonshine songs
they licked his fevered brow
and danced with him
and played with him
through many dogday hours.

    My father told this story
    beside my pillowed bed,
    whispers brown as stubble,
    licks
    upon his head.

The Colour of My Dreams

I'm a really rotten reader
the worst in all the class,
the sort of rotten reader
that makes you want to laugh.

I'm last in all the readin' tests,
my score's not on the page
and when I read to teacher
she gets in such a rage.

She says I cannot form my words
She says I can't build up
and that I don't know phonics
– and don't know c-a-t from k-u-p.

They say that I'm dyslexic
(that's a word they've just found out)
. . . but when I get some plasticine
I know what that's about.

I make these scary monsters
I draw these secret lands
and get my hair all sticky
and paint on all me hands.

I make these super models,
I build these smashing towers
that reach up to the ceiling
and take me hours and hours.

I paint these lovely pictures
in thick green drippy paint
that gets all on the carpet
and makes the cleaners faint.

I build great magic forests,
weave bushes out of string
and paint pink panderellos
and birds that really sing.

I play my world of real believe
I play it every day
and people stand and watch me
but don't know what to say.

They give me diagnostic tests,
they try out reading schemes,
but none of them will ever know
the colour of my dreams.

Praise God For Life

My pal gave me this idea — thanks, Geoff!

Praise God for life
said Mrs Noah
putting on her Sunday
boa . . .
No more cloud
no more rain
I'll hang my washing
out again.

Teacher Goodbye

Our teacher left last Friday;
it was the end of term.
She's going to have a baby
– but said she would return.
We gave her tons of baby things,
we gave her massive cheers.
She looked both sad and happy
and wiped away some tears.
She took away my football cards,
    my chewing gum,
    my sweets,
    the string I use for conkers,
    and a rubber thing that squeaks.
She *said* she'd come to see us,
the baby on her knee.
So I hope she brings the
    football cards
    'cos they belong to me!

Dancing Boy

My sister has a pony
she calls him Dancing Boy
she rides him in the morning
and grooms him every night.
They ride in bright gymkhanas
win silver cups and plates
certificates and medals
badges
brasses
braids . . .

> Dancing Boy is wonderful
> she talks to him each day
> and whispers secret secrets
> in a special pony way.

She draws him pony pictures
she pins them round her bed,
his manger for her pillow
and his stable in her head.

Foolish Robert

Robert with his blow-up boat
thought he'd like to have a float
 and on his own
 with no one there
pumped it up with seaside air.
  'Yo ho,' he laughed
  'I'll have some fun
  sailing in the sea and sun.'
So, on a lovely, sunny day
Robert gently blew away
  whilst waves and seagulls
  off-shore breezes
  softly danced about his kneeses.
'Oh this is fab,' laughed sailor Bobby
boating is a lovely hobby –
  So on he sailed
  bereft of fear
  until the land just disappeared!
'Oh dear,' said Bob
'Where's my mum?
This isn't what I call much fun . . .'
  The waves grew bigger
  the sun went out
  and Robert gave a fearful shout,
'Ahoy!
Oh help
This isn't fair,'
and waved his paddle in the air.

WELL?
What's the end?
I hear you cry
was he saved
or did he die?
The answer is –
I DO NOT KNOW
    but
PLEASE BE CAREFUL
WHERE YOU GO.

Remembering How to
Cross the Road

It is easy to stop
It is easy to wait
It is easy to look left
It is easy to look right
It is easy to look left

again
It is easy to listen
and walk across sensibly.
But, when you are being
chased
by
herds of
Brontosaurus
Diplodocus
Stegosaurus
Styracosaurus
and a boy called Toby Mitchell
then it's hard.

Access

Wheelchair access
mind the crates
wheelchair access
bottles, plates
wheelchair access
find your way
wheelchair access?
Not today.
Wheelchair access
    10.00 – 3.00
wheelchair access?
Don't ask me . . .
    Wheelchair access
    ask the cat
    wheelchair access

    round the back.

Death by Worksheet

Out teacher's worksheet barmy
our school is worksheet mad
she makes the biggest worksheets
the world has ever had.
We fill in all her questions
numbers, words, and dates
adjectives and clauses
(copied from my mates).
She says they 'test our knowledge'
they tell her what we know
who is quick and clever
and who is very slow . . .
      They tell her who remembers
      parts of plants and names
      wires and magnetism
        kings
          and queens
            and reigns.

But I cannot remember
for they say that I am slow
as I gaze beyond the windows
And dream of things I know.

Summer

Apple-dapple summer
apple-dapple time
poppies red as ribbons
daisies white as lime.
Apples, plums and peaches
songbirds in the trees
summer suns are glowing
picnics
ices
teas.

> Apple-dapple summer
> pollen in the breeze
> thistles pricking fingers
> nettles on the knees.
> Noses sore with sneezes
> eyes as red as wine
> summer suns are glowing
> and it's called
> Ahhhhh Tiiiiiisuuuueeee
> time.

Sunbeams on the Telly

Oh no!
      they're at the window again
          weaving
          winking
          laughing
          prancing to get in . . .
It's no good pulling curtains
pretending we're not here
moving screens or sunshades
pulling summer blinds . . .
          They're mean
          they're mad
          they're magic
          They come here day by day
          to dance upon our telly
          on every sunny day.

Mum Says

Mum says that:
If I go straight out after a hot bath
I will catch something
that
I will never get rid of.

Mum says that:
If I watch too much TV,
play music too loud
pick spots,
leave greens,
or pull faces when the wind changes,
I will grow up to look like dad.

So I don't.
It's not worth the risk.

I'd Love to Be . . .

I'd love to be a swordfish
said the mussel to the prawn
I hoped I'd be a swordfish
the day that I was born . . .

But God made me a mussel
and I'm stuck upon these rocks
I never ever travel
and have no shoes or socks.
Oh! I'd love to be a swordfish
a sealion
or a squid
a crab
or dab
or dolphin
a haddock
or a whale.

> But
> I was born a mussel
> we are just who we are,
> my mother thinks I'm lovely
> my mum thinks I'm a . . .
> STAR.

In Memory of Hopscotch

*Did you know that children have been chalking hopscotch
for 400 years? Now teachers ban it!*

With stolen chalk
and shards of clay
we drew our hopscotch
day by day . . .
>milken lines
>Pullman long
>anacondas
>bold and strong . . .
Whirling skirts
grey paved streets
trips and tumbles
stamping feet . . .
>four hundred years
>still skimming on
>ballad, folk tale
>word and song.
Four hundred squares
each a year
spins and twizzles
tears and jeers.
>But spot the ogre
>playground man
>brush and measure
>rule and plan.
Pollute
destroy
let waste abound,
>but never chalk upon the ground.

Games

I like games.
Shane likes games.
We all like games
at our school.
We have games clubs:
    chess and dance and snooker
    table tennis, darts
    computer, flute and singing
    pottery and art.
Shane only likes
    pushing
    shouting
    shoving
    and pulling people over
sort of games.

That's why he had to leave chess club.

Something to Shout About

I like amazing animals
not boring amazing animals
like pink elephants
and cows that jump over the moon.
No, give me amazing animals
that are really
S – P – E – C – I – A – L.
I once saw a rabbit pie
fly
straight into the Chelsea goalmouth
and head a Giggsy
cross
straight into the net!

GOAL!

Now that's what I call something
to shout about.

Poem

(after P.E. lesson)

And now it's time for sensible time,
Everyone on the sensible mat . . .
that's better,
that's much better.
Wayne! We are all having sensible time.
That means you too.
We are not having pushing and tugging of people
    time . . .
Now we all know why we are sitting here, don't we?
No, Jamie it's nothing to do with football
– or your uncle, Hannah.
We are all sitting here because
we have a very important visitor.
We are also sitting here because Paul has lost his
    trousers . . .
and now the poetry man has got to wait
until the person who is wearing Paul's trousers
owns up.
Now all look carefully.
Someone is wearing Paul's trousers.
The poetry man must think we are all very silly
    children.
No, Liza, of course the poetry man hasn't taken Paul's
    trousers.
If we go on being silly
and if we continue wasting the poetry man's time,
he will never read to us
and he will never explain
where he gets all his clever ideas from.

My Father Saw

Just inside the cupboard
    (underneath the stairs)
my father saw a dragon
    saying evening prayers.
He heard the tramp of soldiers
    marching off to war,
a thousand dancing walruses
    and a fairy on the floor.
He smelt the smell of witches
    brewing nasty spells,
a pirate with cutlass,
    a beggar with a bell.
He watched a princess weeping,
    he caught a falling star,
saw a dodo flying
    and a rainbow in a jar.
He heard the angels singing,
    a poet reading rhyme,
a band of robbers laughing
    with tongues as red as wine.

My father always sees things
and it isn't really fair
for when I go to look inside it –
    the cupboard's always bare.

Boxes

Why do we always want to tidy things up?
Clear the bushes,
chop the trees,
lightened darkness,
marina the seas?

Why can't we have bigger and better mud flats,
tangles in the woodlands,
puddles in the park?

I like losing my way
and not being able to find things.
Why can't I look for books
on the wrong shelf,
chalk my own hopscotch,
tick the wrong box
and sing the wrong tune?

So, let me out of the box
    Columbus
    Leonardo
    and Charlie Parker
    never got into.

But most of all abolish
literacy hour.

Seasons

A springtime tale
is best they say –
sunshine creeping in to play,
Easter tadpoles, beans in jars
birds in boxes
brand new cars.

    A summer's tale
    is ringed with flowers
    cottage gardens, sunny hours
    cotton dresses
    cooing doves
    summer sandals
    summer loves.

An autumn tale you cannot see
it's not the sort of time for me –
fog and mist
long dark nights
soggy socks
woolly tights.

    A winter tale's
    is kissed with wine
    frost and snuggles
    logs and fires
    carols, tinsel
    warm deep beds
    Christmas toys
    and sleepy heads.

Wildlife

Why do we say wildlife
when wildlife isn't wild?
    It's mostly soft and gentle,
    it's mostly meek and mild.
We don't see lions bombing
and tigers driving tanks,
platoons of pink flamingos
or regiments of yaks.
We don't see wars of blue whales
or rabbits flying jets,
walruses with shotguns
or parachuting pets.
To me wildlife is gentle
it loves to hide away,
it's mostly shy and silent
it likes to run and play.
    It's really us that's wildlife
    our lifestyle's really wild
    bombs
    and bangs
    and burnings
father, mother, child.

Big Chief Grandad

After breakfast
    lunch
    and tea
grandad would
    slip the catch
    and step
    gently
    into the back yard.
Where's he going?
    I would ask
    fearful of missing some fun.
'He has gone to make water'
I would be told by grandma
in her special voice.
I always felt proud to have a grandfather
who could make water.
A bit like making fire
I supposed –
    but harder.

Insomnia

(a posh word for not being able to go to sleep)

At midnight there are no more sheep
to count.
No more hedges left
or right.

At one o'clock
the cats are in the alley,
the bats are in the eves
the rats are in the rafters,
. . . the nightingales in the trees.

I lay silent
with Ted
in somnia.

Index of First Lines

Naomi House

Naomi House was built just over ten years ago to provide children with life-limiting conditions a place to go where they could receive specialist care and support.

The hospice is an environment that enables the children, and their families, to experience things such as swimming and outings, that might not be possible ordinarily. Over and above this, the team at Naomi House strives to give the families support through all the phases of a child's illness, which means that we offer respite care, end-of-life care and bereavement support. Here at Naomi House our specialist nurses and care staff aim to give one-to-one care to the children who visit, allowing parents and brothers and sisters time to relax.

Over the last few years medical advances mean that many of the children who visit Naomi House will live beyond their teenage years to become young adults. In 2007 we announced an appeal to raise £12 million to build, equip and run *jacksplace@naomihouse*, a hospice for young people aged between fourteen and twenty-five years old that will satisfy their specific needs.

We have spent a lot of time with the young people who will use the hospice, to make sure that the building includes the things that are important to them. They had some really good ideas, like large bedrooms where they can meet their friends to play music, watch dvds or play computer games, a cinema area and en-suite bathrooms. Other very important facilities will include a hydrotherapy pool and a treatment room. All the design aspects of the hospice aim to give the young people independence, privacy and dignity.

Our appeal got off to a great start in 2007 with an amazing legacy donation of £6 million from Jack Witham. Since then we have been busy in the local communities raising further funds.

Last autumn our campaign received a big boost when Andy Burrows came to visit Naomi House to find out what we are trying to achieve. Since then Andy has taken Naomi House to his heart, and we have been overwhelmed by the support he is giving us by dedicating his album *Colour of My Dreams* to Naomi House. The combination of the poetry by Peter and the music by Andy is magical. We are delighted with the huge amount of support and kindness that has been shown by everyone involved.

If you would like to know more about *jacksplace@naomihouse*, please visit: *www.naomihouse.org.uk*

I'd Rather Be a FOOTBALLER

Poems by Paul Cookson

Paul Cookson's greatest hits! This book is the essential Paul Cookson collection, featuring his most popular poems, including 'Superman's Dogs', 'The Toilet Seat Has Teeth', 'Let No One Steal Your Dreams' and 'The Amazing Captain Concorde'.

Short Visit, Long Stay

Out school trip was a special occasion
But we never reached our destination
Instead of the zoo
I was locked in the loo
Of an M62 service station.

The TRUTH about TEACHERS

Hilarious rhymes By Paul Cookson, David Harmer, Brian Moses anD Roger Stevens

Bestselling poets Paul, David, Brian and Roger are all ex-teachers and the perfect people to reveal what goes on inside the staffroom. You'll find out what makes your teachers tick and what they get up to at the weekend. After all, there is a lot more to your mild-mannered maths teacher than meets the eye . . .

It's a Definite Sign

Our dinner lady Mrs Mack
Is well in love with Mr Fipps
Because at every dinner time
She winks and smiles when he's in line
And gives him extra chips.

Paul Cookson

Funny poems chosen by Fiona Waters

Smile! This is a very sunny, happy collection of poems from an expert anthologist, and is guaranteed to bring laughter into your day.

The Laughter Forecast

Today will be humorous
With some giggly patches,
Scattered outbreaks of chuckling in the south
And smiles spreading from the east later,
Widespread chortling
Increasing to gale-force guffaws towards evening.
The outlook for tomorrow
Is hysterical.

Sue Cowling

A selected list of titles available from Macmillan Children's Books

The prices shown below are correct at the time of going to press. However, Macmillan Publishers reserves the right to show new retail prices on covers, which may differ from those previously advertised.

I'd Rather Be a Footballer Poems by Paul Cookson	978-0-330-45713-2	£4.99
The Truth About Teachers Hilarious rhymes by Paul Cookson, David Harmer, Brian Moses and Roger Stevens	978-0-330-44723-2	£4.99
Laugh Out Loud Funny poems chosen by Fiona Waters	978-0-330-45456-8	£4.99
Why Otters Don't Wear Socks Poems by Roger Stevens	978-0-330-44851-2	£3.99

All Pan Macmillan titles can be ordered from our website, www.panmacmillan.com, or from your local bookshop and are also available by post from:

Bookpost, PO Box 29, Douglas, Isle of Man IM99 1BQ

Credit cards accepted. For details:
Telephone: 01624 677237
Fax: 01624 670923
Email: bookshop@enterprise.net
www.bookpost.co.uk

Free postage and packing in the United Kingdom